Performance Management

Developing People and Performance

Frank Scott-Lennon
& Fergus Barry

Acknowledgements

We are most grateful to many, many managers – too numerous to mention – within various organisations; their ideas and practice have greatly informed our thinking and our view of Best Practice.

We are also most grateful to those managers who read earlier drafts of this book and who enriched us with their insights.

We are greatly indebted to Wayne Brockbank, Charles Spinoza and Paul Sparrow for taking the time to read the book and provide us with such wonderful endorsements.

We particularly wish to thank our wives, Claire and Maria, for their continuing support; without it this book, and all of our other work, would be far less rich.

Frank Scott-Lennon
Fergus Barry

December 2008

ISBN 0-9519738-2-7
ISBN 978-0-9519738-2-0

All design, art work and liaison with printers has been undertaken by Neworld Associates, 9 Greenmount Avenue, Harold's Cross, Dublin 12.

Publisher: Managements Briefs, 30 The Palms, Clonskeagh, Dublin 14.

Table of Contents

Chapter	Description	Page
1	**Why Performance Management?** → Developing a Performance Management Culture → Objectives of a Performance Management System (PMS) → Role of the Line Manager in successful PMSs → Motivational benefits of a PMS → The Ten 'Performance Commandments'	1
2	**The D E F T Model of Performance Management** → Dialogue between each Manager and his/her employee → Expectations about the requirements of the job → Feedback on performance → Timely treatment of the first three components of the D E F T model	7
3	**D E F T – Dialogue** → Dialogue as the foundation of PMS → Building trust levels → Dialogue as an aid to coaching behaviours → Getting joint agreement on critical areas of job responsibility → Overcoming defensiveness → A two-way process	15
4	**D E F T – Expectations of Performance** → Clarification of expectations → Linking to Divisional/Corporate goals → Establishing Key Result Areas that focus on results → Collaboration and active involvement in goal setting → Skills for goal setting	25

Chapter	Description	Page
5	**DEFT – Feedback** → Feedback as an on-going process → Linking to agreed KRAs and goals → Preparing for the session → Structured format for feedback sessions → Tips for giving and receiving feedback → Exploring positive and constructive feedback → Commitment for follow-through	37
6	**DEFT – Timely Approach** → Integrating PMS with other core organisation systems → Feedback should be close to the event → Regular reviews within PMS → Tips for interim and annual reviews → Sample timetable for phases of PMS → Ensuring the provision of enabling conditions for success of PMS	47
7	**People Development Commitments** → Creating a positive climate for people growth → Focus on organisational needs → Insights on personal development within PMS → Alternative development opportunities within organisations → Integration with Organisation Training and Development plan → Follow-through on commitments	55
8	**Competencies: A Key Approach to People Development** → Focus on 'how' the job is to be done → Competency development and high performance → How to build Competency based approaches to people development → Values for competency approaches → Coaching for personal development	63

Chapter	Description	Page
9	**Linking Performance to Reward** → Linking performance and pay across an organisation → Complexity of pay for performance → Rewarding behaviours and achievement → Decisions on 'weighting' of reward criteria → Consistency and fairness of reward	77
10	**Critical Success Factors** → Role of top management → Line of sight to Organisation goals → Integration of PMS with Organisation systems → Participative dialogue → Quality Feedback skills → Best practice coaching and training → Consistency of application → Regular recognition of good performance → Personal development → Managers 'make the call' → Excellent follow-through mechanisms	87
A	**Appendix** → Appendix I – Template of Simple Performance Management 'Form' → Appendix II – Sample Template for the Structure of Performance Discussions	97

Foreword

This book captures all of the elements of current Best Practice Performance Management.

It is a very welcome edition to a developing series of Human Resource, Organisation Behaviour and General Management Books.

All of the books in the series aim to capture the essentials for busy managers; essential knowledge and skill presented in an accessible easy-to-read style.

A list of books already published within the series appears on the inside of the back cover; our website www.ManagementBriefs.com lists forthcoming titles.

We welcome any contact from you the reader; it will only improve our products and our connection to our reader population.

Frank Scott-Lennon
Series Editor
frank@ManagementBriefs.com

December 2008

1

Why Performance Management?

Chapter 1 outline

Why Performance Management?

- → Developing a Performance Management Culture
- → Objectives of a Performance Management System (PMS)
- → Role of the Line Manager in successful PMSs
- → Motivational benefits of a PMS
- → The Ten 'Performance Commandments'

Introduction

The performance of key people in an organisation determines whether or not that organisation succeeds within its marketplace. To create real stakeholder value organisations need to develop high performance cultures which are strong on:

- Clarity about objectives and goals
- Continuous assessment and the provision of honest feedback
- Recognition of good performance
- The enhancement of individual's competencies
- The development of team/ organisational capability

The development of such a high performance culture is facilitated by the existence of an integrated, simple and easy-to-operate Performance Management System (PMS).

The task of reviewing the performance of individuals within organisations is a line management function and thus should be clearly seen as a general management system – indeed as a core system for achieving the organisation's objectives. It is the foundation of the basic architecture of management.

It is difficult to see the role of a manager as not having a very strong leadership responsibility which can only achieve true expression through a good PMS.

It is possible to have multiple objectives for a PMS but organisations should not have too many objectives. Limiting the objectives to a small number will facilitate focus for the organisation. The specific objectives chosen will need to be tailored in each instance to the requirements of the organisation. Nonetheless, it is possible to indicate that most management teams would include the following three major objectives for their PMS:

- → The improvement of individual performance
- → The personal development of the individual employee
- → The development of balanced team capability

Including these three objectives has the benefit of demonstrating clearly to all that the PMS has something for everyone in the organisation. For the management team, it has the particular benefit of improved individual and team performance and thereby organisational performance. For the employee, the PMS offers a realistic opportunity for the achievement of agreed goals and for personal development.

The role of a manager has a very strong leadership responsibility which can only achieve true expression through a good PMS. This is because such a system will clearly focus individuals on business needs, organisational goals and developing individual, team and organisational capability. A well-developed PMS should be guide and scaffold to the manager as she/he sets about leading his/her staff in a direction consistent with where the organisation wishes to go.

The PMS also provides a motivational context for individuals and teams in organisations. It does this by capitalising on the motivational benefit of agreeing meaningful goals with individuals and teams; these goals therefore become a motivational target for individuals. Further motivational value can be obtained through monitoring the attainment of the goals and then providing good quality feedback during and at the end of the review period.

A key element in this leadership and motivational aspect of the manager's job is that the PMS should provide a clear focus on performance metrics, without which it is extremely difficult to measure performance or to provide feedback on same.

There are a few simple basics (our Ten Performance Commandments) that have been distilled from the myriad of ideas and research that has focussed on improving human performance in business and in sport. These ways of improving performance are listed below.

Panel 1.1

The Ten Performance Commandments

1. Goal-setting
2. Performer involvement in setting goals
3. Creating a 'line of sight' to the organisational goals and agreeing explicitly the individual's commitments to the team
4. Contracting with the coach to provide the support required by the performer improves performer confidence and performance
5. Feedback at regular intervals
6. Coach/Performer dialogue on insights provided by the feedback
7. Recognising effort and results
8. Regular reviews of results achieved and competencies demonstrated
9. Equity in the management of performance improves organisational performance
10. Aligning consequences with goal achievement

When mentioning consequences we should indicate that a good PMS provides the opportunity to make a very clear link between performance and remuneration, a link that is not always sufficiently clear in organisations. It is our experience that in the first instance managers must become fully familiar with all aspects of the operation of a PMS prior to directly linking same to remuneration.

The sub-title of this book focuses on developing people as well as performance. All good PMSs place a heavy emphasis on the development of individuals' competencies. These include the values/cultural behaviours as well as the technical/functional knowledge and skills, particularly in relation to the current job and possible future positions within the organisation.

2

The D E F T Model of Performance Management

D – Dialogue
E – Expectations
F – Feedback
T – Timely Approach

Chapter 2 outline
The D E F T Model of Performance Management

- → Dialogue between each Manager and his/her employee
- → Expectations about the requirements of the job
- → Feedback on performance
- → Timely treatment of the first three components of the D E F T model

Introduction

We present in this short chapter a brief overview of the D E F T Model of Performance Management; each element described will be treated in later chapters.

DIALOGUE is at the core of the PMS process. The dialogue between each manager and his/her direct report is the most critical part of successful management. The candour and honesty of this dialogue is at the core of successful performance management. The initial dialogue meeting is perhaps the most important part of our model of performance management; this is the first opportunity for the planning of goal achievement and personal development. It is vitally important because at this initial stage we would stress that performance management has very, very little to do with the completion of forms. Research suggests that circa 50% of performance management systems are **not** effective. This is usually due to the fact that they are form focussed and what are called 'tick and flick' systems. This usually reflects the fact that the process is seen as an 'add on' by the line managers rather than an integral part of how they manage their own people.

Dialogue is at the core of the PMS process. The dialogue between each manager and his/her direct report is the most critical part of successful management.

An effective system has on the other hand everything to do with creating a climate for meaningful dialogue between a leader and team member at the commencement of a performance management review period and during same. Some managers suggest that within their busy jobs they do not have time for the level of dialogue required; we hope that in our next chapter, when we focus exclusively on dialogue, we will be able to justify how beneficial it can be. However, every manager must understand that his/her core role is to achieve results through and with people and to build the capability of each employee and the team; this may only be done through meaningful dialogue.

EXPECTATIONS about the requirements of the job are the principal subject matter for this dialogue between the line manager and his/her team member. Every effort should be made to clarify the expectations that each has in respect of the job that is required to be done.

As hinted earlier when treating dialogue above, it is imperative that this process is essentially a jointly driven process; as we will show later, this will principally revolve around the establishment

Panel 2.1

A Way of Looking at Expectations

Expectations must be totally clear in three distinct areas:

---

1. What the individual is expected to personally achieve, the individual's expected contribution at a strategic and functional level and commitments in the support of other team members - the *'WHAT'.*
2. The behaviours both cultural and technical that the individual is to develop and demonstrate in order to achieve the above - the *'HOW'*.
3. The agreed coaching level and actual support and resources (including training and development) that the manager is going to deliver to empower the performer to achieve – the *'SUPPORT'.*

of the key result areas for the job and the goals or objectives that are to be attained within each of those key result areas. We will provide a full treatment of these expectations of performance in chapter 4.

FEEDBACK is an essential ingredient for a good PMS. In its simplest terms it is an opportunity for both parties to explore how they believe the team member is performing against the expectations that have been earlier clarified; it also provides an opportunity for discussing progress with these expectations on a regular basis and for focusing on the personal development of the team member. We provide some further insights on this feedback process within Chapter 5.

TIMELY treatment of each of the above elements of the PMS is critical. Thus the clarification of expectations should be undertaken at a meaningful time within the business cycle of the organisation. It is also important that feedback is not given in a quick once-a-year setting but is an on-going regular part of the dialogue that should take place between team leader and team member. If this is not happening on an on-going basis the PMS

Panel 2.2

Recent implementation of a PMS – *a D E F T experience!*

A company in the financial services sector wished to totally re-vamp an over-complicated PMS that had fallen into disrepute within the organisation and they did so by utilising **D E F T** in the following way:

- → Conducted an organisation-wide critique of the existing system
- → Built on this critique to launch a **D E F T** approach to PMS
- → Decided at the outset to have no fanfare launch, forms, booklets or formal training sessions along the usual lines
- → PMS was announced at successive management meetings across the organisation as part of the business of those meetings; it was stressed that the process would be a simple one-page approach to **D E F T** which would commence in two months
- → **D E F T** will be integrated with budget preparation activity over the next two months
- → Also announced that one hour would be taken at each of the next three management meetings across the organisation to provide more details of **D E F T** and to coach/train managers in the requisite skills
- → Clarified with these teams that this approach was being used to achieve the required consistency of goal setting across the team and across the organisation
- → The consistent application of **D E F T** would be on the agenda every two months at said management meetings across the organisation

This particular organisation is two and a half years on from launch and has developed within the organisation a most successful implementation of **D E F T**.

will not be effective. The effective PMS then is reflected in how we personally manage – it is not an 'add on' form filling exercise. If the manager contracts effectively with the employee and then plans the formal and informal dialogues, he/she will begin to manage through the PMS process rather than add the process to how he/she manages. Effectively handled he/she can save valuable management time through this investment in good management.

There is no more successful way of bedding down a PMS in an organisation than by having all organisation members see that the system is alive and well at the senior management table.

In this very brief introductory treatment of **D E F T** we have not yet mentioned the importance of metrics within a good PMS. It is probably already apparent to the reader that best practice goal setting will have both quantitative and qualitative measures which again should be linked into the primary business metrics. This is one of the most difficult aspects of a PMS and we will give detailed treatment to performance metrics in Chapter 4.

A final note that we must include in this early treatment of **D E F T** is that at its optimum it is a top-down process. There is no more successful way of bedding down a PMS in an organisation than by having all organisation members see that the system is alive and well at the senior management table. Another aspect of the top down approach is that senior and middle managers should champion the system in such a way that they are seen to be regularly and openly enthusiastic about how beneficial the PMS is to the business. As mentioned earlier this will be all the more meaningful if the clarification of expectations is clearly linked into business priorities. Even more important is the basic reality that where a manager has seen his/her manager carry out a worthwhile expectations dialogue, he/she is then much more likely to have the confidence, competence and commitment to deliver an effective dialogue with his/her own team members – this process is known as 'modelling'.

Over the coming four chapters we will look at each of these four phases in turn, starting in Chapter 3 with 'Dialogue'.

Summary of chapter 2

The D E F T Model of Performance Management

→ **D E F T** is the model for successful PMS – At its core are **Dialogue, Expectations** & **Feedback**. All must be completed in a **Timely** manner

→ **Dialogue** is at the heart of the process; it involves 'engaging' and explaining the essentials for job/role success

→ **Candour** and **open communication** are at the core of a successful PMS

→ **Expectations**, when clarified well through KRAs and Goals, give motivational direction and provide the context for performance improvement in the period ahead

→ **Feedback** must be regular and focused on performance against expectations and also on skill/competency enhancement

→ **Timely** treatment of each of the above elements is critical - PMS must become part of 'how we manage' day by day, month by month....not just a 'once-a-year' exercise

→ PMS must be a **top-down process** that delivers commitment to the process at all levels within the organisation

→ **Senior management in particular must model best practice dialogue**, clarification of expectations and feedback as they carry out the process of PM with their teams and beyond

D E F T – Dialogue

3

D – Dialogue
E – Expectations
F – Feedback
T – Timely Approach

Chapter outline

DEFT – Dialogue

- → Dialogue as the foundation of PMS
- → Building trust levels
- → Dialogue as an aid to coaching behaviours
- → Getting joint agreement on critical areas of job responsibility
- → Overcoming defensiveness
- → A two-way process

Introduction

DIALOGUE is the foundation on which a good PMS is built. Good dialogue is made easier when an open trusting relationship exists between two individuals; thus enlightened managers and team members should work hard at building trust levels. However, when sometimes there are issues that need to be addressed or less than perfect trust levels, it is better to acknowledge that reality.

Having built trust levels the dialogue must still set expectations around the:

1. Role
2. Goals
3. Professional standards of behaviour and relationships required to achieve business performance

We are not talking here only about good dialogue being maintained in the day-to-day cut and trust of carrying out one's job. We are in fact talking about taking time out from this often frenetic activity to reflect for a short time on the priorities within the job and ensuring that they are being attended to in a measured way. This is where the manager becomes coach. Critical to this is the coaching skill of the manager allied to the performance insights he/she delivers much like a golf professional to a client. The first priority is to identify those behaviours that are producing positive results and also identify the behaviours (or lack of them) that are not producing the desired results. Having done this the coach suggests practice and training skills to improve performance and finally hands over responsibility for delivering the changed performance to the performer.

> The objective of this dialogue is to get joint agreement on what are the critical areas on which to focus the job knowledge, energy and skills of the team member.

The objective of this dialogue is to get joint agreement on what are the critical areas on which to focus the job knowledge, energy and skills of the team member. Thus it has not alone to embody a good review of the priorities and activities but to achieve as far as possible joint agreement on these issues. It may not be possible in all instances to have a total oneness of mind and therefore the manager from time to time may have to use optimal influencing skills to bring the team member to the view that some aspect(s) of the job is in fact critical. If the team member cannot be brought to this view then the manager must direct the individual to achieve against reasonable goals, providing clarity of consequences where the individual rejects coaching and still does not achieve.

As hinted in the reference above to a trusting relationship, it is really important that this dialogue takes place in as open and non-defensive a manner as possible. If either party enter into the dialogue in a defensive mode then it is unlikely that the objectives of the dialogue will be fully achieved. The manager leading this dialogue bears the primary responsibility to model this open non-defensive mode. The manager should seek to create

Panel 3.1

Sample dialogue at outset of PMS

- → Arrange initial meeting with team member
- → Explore business and organisation realities and identify the contribution required over the coming period within the particular organisation/division/section
- → Indicate that one wishes to utilise **D E F T** as a focusing process
- → Briefly explain components of **D E F T** and demonstrate how it can be linked to business direction
- → Stress that it is not about form-filling – any paperwork/form that we use is just an important record of our commitments to each other
- → Ask the individual to explore what they can contribute to achieving the requirements for the section and explore how they need to change their behaviours and develop new competencies to achieve the new requirements.
- → Ask the individual to review their career aspirations and plans
- → Can we meet next week to discuss from both our viewpoints?
  - Key Result Areas of importance which will include your contribution to strategic goals, stewardship/ functional role goals and the key commitments you will have as a team member to support others to achieve.
  - Some things we want to achieve within those areas
  - Any immediate and/or long-term development issues

Panel 3.2

Active Listening

Active Listening involves taking positive steps to fully 'hear' the other person with understanding.

Exercise for developing your **ACTIVE LISTENING** skills in a context where you realise that these skills should be improved

- → Identify a meeting in which you have a significant point to put across, but where there are opposing views
- → Discern specific **ACTIVE LISTENING** behaviours that you would like to engage in to ensure that you 'hear' fully the other's views
- → Such behaviours could be:
  - Repeating a shortened version of what has been said
  - Checking for understanding
  - Reflecting back to the other your sense of their underlying feelings
  - Demonstrating listening attentiveness through body language
- → Contract with a colleague at the meeting to observe your behaviour and to provide you with some feedback after the meeting
- → Listen to and reflect on the feedback
- → Build on positives and put in place further opportunities to improve any non-listening behaviours that were evident
- → Repeat the above in other situations and build on the feedback and further develop your **ACTIVE LISTENING** skills – such skill development will serve you well in many influencing situations, including performance discussions

that relationship by explaining why the expectations are required and the importance of the individual's contribution to group and organisational success.

It should be noted that at no stage have we really laid emphasis on forms for a PMS. This is because we believe it is absolutely critical that the principle of dialogue we are treating in this chapter is so paramount that participants within a PMS should concentrate on the dialogue and only use the form as a record their commitments. Indeed it is our experience that in many organisations the use of over-complicated forms in actual fact gets in the way of successful dialogue and a good PMS. Thus the dialogue that we are speaking about is much closer being recorded on a concise one- or two-page form or, as is the case in a rising number of organisations, recorded on line on a short customised form. Organisations which currently use an extensive form in respect of their PMS should rigorously examine whether or not there are elements of the form that get in the way of a successful PMS. Many organisations in recent years have come back from such complicated forms to close to the blank page idea where they have just one or two pages which really only focus on expectations and personal development. We provide an example of such a simple form as Appendix I.

Indeed it is our experience that in many organisations the use of over-complicated forms in actual fact gets in the way of successful dialogue and a good PMS.

We have not yet stressed that dialogue is really a two-way process which involves the skill of ACTIVE LISTENING as well as ASSERTIVENESS. This points the way to developing further one's listening and assertiveness skills if one wishes to have a successful dialogue process within D E F T as the foundation of a good PMS.

Skill development is rooted in finding opportunities to complete exercises similar to those within Panels 3.2 left and 3.3 overleaf. All the better if one can use a coach or trusted colleague to de-brief one's attempts to build additional skills into one's repertoire.

Panel 3.3

Assertiveness

Assertiveness involves being capable of clearly stating your needs without in any way offending the other person.

Exercise for developing your **ASSERTIVENESS** skills in a context where you realise that these skills should be improved

- Choose either an organisational or social setting where an interaction of more than two people will occur
- Decide on some specific **ASSERTIVE** behaviours that you would like to engage in when getting your view across to the other(s)
- Such behaviours could be
  - Clearly stating your needs
  - Being confident about your rights
  - Empathetically listening to resistance without interruption
  - Firmly saying 'no' when appropriate
  - Re-asserting your position
- Contract with a colleague or friend to observe your behaviour and to provide you with some feedback after the interaction
- Listen to and reflect on the feedback
- Build on positives and put in place further opportunities to improve any behaviours that were insufficiently **ASSERTIVE** or any which might have bordered on the aggressive
- Repeat the above in other situations and build on the feedback and further develop your **ASSERTIVENESS** skills - such skill development will serve you well in many influencing situations, including performance discussions

We will now proceed to treating 'Expectations' in our next Chapter.

Summary of Chapter 3

D E F T - Dialogue

→ Dialogue, which should be **open, honest and trusting**, is the foundation on which PMS is built

→ Dialogue, in its purest PMS form, regularly takes time out from the busyness of day-to-day operations to **discuss issues that aid focus** on the job and improved performance

→ **Dialogue is a joint exercise** of providing role clarity going forward, utilising the expectations and feedback phases of the **D E F T** model

→ Positive coaching requires key performance insights and **a desire to build on the positive** whilst not ignoring areas for improvement

→ Optimum dialogue demands **non-defensive behaviour** from all participants

→ PMS **forms are secondary to the process** of dialogue; they are really only useful if they are short – be that in hard copy or on-line

→ Dialogue demands good **LISTENING** and **ASSERTIVENESS** skills, which we can improve with practice

4 DEFT – Expectations of Performance

D – Dialogue
E – Expectations
F – Feedback
T – Timely Approach

Chapter outline

DEFT – Expectations of Performance

- → Clarification of expectations
- → Linking to Divisional/Corporate goals
- → Establishing Key Result Areas that focus on results
- → Collaboration and active involvement in goal setting
- → Skills for goal setting

Introduction

If dialogue, as treated in the previous chapter, is the principal process within a good PMS then the clarification of EXPECTATIONS is the bedrock of such a system; it is the foundation on which all else is build. As mentioned earlier the clarification of expectations involves initially focusing on Job Purpose and Key Result Areas (KRAs), ensuring that they have a clear 'line of sight' to divisional and corporate strategic objectives or a balanced scorecard, as used by many organisations; then one focuses on setting goals within these KRAs.

Effectiveness is a basic pre-requisite for a successful manager. In order to be effective a manager must 'do the right things', rather than 'do things right'. The guidance for what is the right thing comes from the corporate strategy. In some organisations this will be translated into results focussed business plans or into a balanced scorecard which itemises the key corporate goals under the headings of:

→ Customer/Market Goals

→ Financial Goals

→ Process Improvement Goals

→ People/Team Development Goals

It is of little benefit if the manager is very efficient but is in fact driving down the wrong track, as it were. The role of the leader is to share context and make meaning of the corporate imperatives or scorecard for his/her team. The best way of ensuring that one is putting one's energy into the vital rather than peripheral elements of the job is to spend some time clearly establishing:

1. The Corporate Strategic Goals or Corporate Scorecard
2. The Divisional Scorecard or Strategic Requirements
3. The Team Priority objectives if one and two are to be achieved
4. The basic job/role purpose of the individual in one or two sentences
5. The Key Result Areas of the job.

In agreeing KRAs the team leader and team member should focus on the 'line of sight' to divisional and corporate goals and those areas of the job in which it is critical to achieve meaningful results. Thus the KRAs should be seen not as any fancy add-ons to the job but as areas in which it is essential to focus for success in the job. One of the best ways of initially grasping this idea might be through a sporting analogy. Envision those areas of importance that a coach/manager/ captain of a team would hold in front of that team as being really critical areas on which to focus if they are to succeed in whatever championship they are preparing for; see panel 4.1 for a sample set of KRAs for such a team.

Panel 4.1

Sample sporting team KRAs

- → Attack
- → Defence
- → Positional gains
- → Scoring
- → Communication
- → Set-pieces
- → Knowledge of opposition
- → Tactics
- → Motivation
- → Individual skill development
- → Individual fitness
- → Teamwork contribution
- → Discipline
- → Territorial gain/advantage

It should be noted in the example within Panel 4.1 that one could categorise the KRAs that are listed as either being technical or soft, even though some KRAs could have a foot in both camps, as it were. Thus one could see that for example Fitness, Set-pieces and Scoring are very definitely technical whereas Teamwork, Communication and Discipline are somewhat softer. It is important for staff in organisations to realise that their jobs have these two aspects as well. Thus a manager approaching the task of drafting her/his KRAs must realise that there may well be a predominance of technical type KRAs; however each manager's job will also have soft KRAs as well, perhaps two or three within the six to nine KRAs that each manager should have.

KRAs focus on results rather than on activities or tasks. Thus in trying to establish KRAs the manager should not focus on the day-to-day inputs that are made but should rather try to ascertain the important results that should derive from the activities within the job.

A Production Manager, for example, would have one KRA, among others, that would be related to the number of units produced; likewise he/she would have another KRA related to the quality of the finished product.

When establishing KRAs for these two responsibilities it would suffice to state that the relevant KRAs are those of 'Output' and 'Quality'.

No mention would be made at this stage of the methods by which results would be achieved; methods will be discussed at a later stage.

Goal setting within these key result areas is the next stage in a successful PMS. It is our experience that it is a skill not always well-honed within managers. Thus it may be that during the course of normal management meetings some skill can be transferred to managers within a very short timeframe along the following lines.

Goal setting should first be seen as a process that should provide goals that are **SMART**:

- → Specific
- → Measurable
- → Achievable
- → Realistic
- → Time-framed

...but above all they should in the vast majority of cases be **jointly agreed and achievement of them should be linked to concrete measures and consequences**.

Panel 4.2

Sample KRAs for Production Manager would include:

- → Output – Product/Service A, B,C etc
- → Quality – Product/Service A,B,C etc
- → Wastage/Rework
- → Lean Initiatives
- → Teamwork Commitments
- → Materials
- → MIS/OIS
- → Budgets
- → Job knowledge
- → Empowerment
- → Performance Management
- → Process control
- → Communication

It is often thought that the period for setting goals should be for a year; but this may not be the best approach. Many firms are now moving to quarterly goal setting. They see the advantage of this in ensuring that every week in every quarter matters. We believe that one should set goals for the short-, medium- and long-term as appropriate to the situation in which one finds oneself. Thus if it is possible to achieve some goal within two months or six months, then that goal should include such a time-based measure. One of the advantages of this approach is that one is providing opportunity for short-/ medium-term achievement which can be a motivator for individuals; all the more so if one positively rewards such achievement at mini-reviews through the year. Panel 4.3 shows possible duration/term of goals.

It is perhaps helpful for managers to view the setting of goals initially from a structural viewpoint, where a particular goal is seen to have a beginning, middle and end.

The **beginning** should always be an active verb, a verb that implies doing either now or in the future. Examples of such verbs could be DEVISE, IMPLEMENT, REDUCE, PRODUCE, INTRODUCE, DEVELOP etc.

Structurally the **end** of these goals is where the measures are put into the process and these measures can be either quantitative or qualitative. Quantitative measures are usually numbers, percentages or timeframes. Qualitative measures, which are most often harder to set, can be aided by the use of phrases such as '... to the extent that...' or '...to the satisfaction of...'.

Panel 4.3

Duration/term of goals

Phase	Possible duration/ term of goal setting
Short-term	1-3 months
Medium-term	4-8 months
Long-term	9-18 months

Lastly the middle part of goals will actually be the 'WHAT', that is what it is you want to deliver, develop, produce etc. written with as much detail as is required for full clarity for the team member.

One of the hardest parts about goal setting is writing them in a manner where they are specific and measurable. Succeeding in doing so will make both the target clearer for the individual and also make the review process easier. The measurement difficulties that would exist with the following goals are easily seen both from the focus and review viewpoints:

→ 'Improve sales for the company' = **POOR GOAL**

→ 'Make changes to product quality' = **POOR GOAL**

The measurement of goals is improved by being quite specific and also by using a timeframe within which the goal must be achieved.

→ 'Increase sales turnover in our retail outlets by 5 per cent over the next six months ensuring that 50% of this increase is in our furniture products' = **GOOD GOAL**

→ 'Identify three improvements that could be made to product quality and implement same prior to end of next quarter' = **GOOD GOAL**

The second set of goals above are more meaningful both for the individual and the organisation insofar as they provide a clear focus for performance and, as they are unambiguous, they will be a more helpful goal come review time.

Not all goals can be expressed in measurable terms quite as easily. Goals within the qualitative areas such as leadership and motivational KRAs, are less easy to express in quantitative terms. A useful technique for the measuring of such goals is to question oneself about the behaviour that will be evident within the organisation if one is focusing/not focusing well on that KRA. Utilising this technique will generate a number of areas of potential progress or dissatisfaction; it will be possible to set goals that re-enforce or turn around behaviour in these areas, which in turn will contribute to improving performance. See the example in Panel 4.4 overleaf.

The measurement of goals within these softer KRAs could be seen to not meet our criteria of being specific and measurable if the goal were as follows:

→ 'Improve Employee Relations within the department' = **POOR GOAL**

→ 'Improve employee commitment' = **POOR GOAL**

An alternative approach would be to focus on some elements of poor Employee Relations that one wishes to improve and then embodying same in a stated goal, such as the following:

→ 'Reduce by 20% the number of occasions when grievances go for resolution above the first line manager; reduce by 25% the total number of grievances within the department'
= **GOOD GOAL**

→ 'Improve employee engagement to a score of 97% by year-end as measured by our engagement algorithm which includes the absenteeism, project achievement and attrition ratios'
= **GOOD GOAL**

Panel 4.4

Tips for goal setting within difficult KRAs

The context is where one wants to set some goals within the KRA of 'Teamwork'

→ As one initially approaches this task, it may appear difficult to write specific goals

→ Then... stop the clock, as it were, ...and think of those areas in which things might go wrong if one was not attending to Teamwork

→ Think specifically of what we would see (the actual visible behaviours)

→ This process might generate issues such as:

- Lack of direction within the team
- Duplication or overlapping of tasks
- Interpersonal conflicts within the team
- Poor 'customer service' behaviours

→ It is then possible to set goals in some or all of the above, which will undoubtedly contribute to an improvement in Teamwork

Note: This technique is not alone useful for a 'blank' that one might have with qualitative KRAs, but the technique is also useful with quantitative KRAs; further examples of this technique can be seen within Panel 4.5

Panel 4.5

Setting goals in softer Key Result Areas - examples

	Teamwork	Delegation
Step 1 **Question what might be going wrong if one is not attending to that area?**	→ Lack of focus/direction → Disorganisation → Conflict → Poor communication	→ Over-burdened manager/team leader → Poor development of team members → Much of the work being done by "the few" → Time-management problems
Step 2 **Now write a goal or two based on correcting or preventing what you have said might be wrong if you were not focussing on that KRA**	→ Arrange initial team meeting to build better focus/ direction, to the extent that directional clarity is established for team → Arrange monthly team meeting to focus exclusively on process improvements in conflict reduction and communication, to the extent that improvements are made on both to the satisfaction of team members	→ Identify two bits of own job that can be delegated and plan the process (of delegation) within one month → Identify two team members and delegate relevant "bits" to them through discussion, coaching and monitoring, to the extent that the job gets done and the individuals experience development

Notwithstanding the fact that it is necessary to set goals that are attainable, it must be stressed that complacency should not be allowed to creep into the PMS by making the goals altogether too cosy. We should not lose sight of the fact that one of the prime objectives for a successful PMS is the improvement of individual performance. The learning curve is an aspect of all organisational activity and, given recent research on the learning organisation, it is clear that each organisation

Performance improvement applies equally to the good performer as it does to the poor performer, if not more so.

should focus on the learning curve and integrate it with the PMS; an organisation will do this best by establishing what it has learned each year and then use that new capability to improve performance year on year. If we cannot do this the organisation is not learning and will eventually be outpaced by its competitive rivals or its stakeholders will soon identify the loss of value added. Thus individuals need to have their skills and abilities stretched that little bit extra as the goals are re-set for the following period. The leader must seriously question things if this cannot happen.

Performance improvement applies equally to the good performer as it does to the poor performer, if not more so. It could thus be argued that in productivity terms it is more beneficial for the organisation to concentrate on stretching the performance of good performers than to do so with poor performers – although this should not be used as an argument not to pursue the required performance improvement of poor performers. If we are to have equity and organisational justice it is critical that non-performers are tackled. The zone of comfort for the non-performer needs to be limited if an organisation is to motivate the majority of its people to perform. When non-performance arises the alarms should 'go off' and a positive coaching style should be immediately engaged to salvage the situation. If this does not get a positive response from the individual a more directive coaching approach should be used and where this fails the disciplinary code should be the next and obvious port of call. At all times managers should coach and counsel to salvage performance that is not fully up to expectations but should also record progress or lack of same lest one needs to move into the disciplinary process at a later time.

This stretching of performance can play a very important part in creating a performance culture within an organisation; key elements within the development of such a culture will be treated at a later stage within this book.

As a final stream of thought in respect of goal setting, managers should ensure that the goals for their team members are where possible fully agreed with them. The purpose of striving for such agreement is to increase the commitment of the team member to the goals: individuals will feel greater ownership of goals when they have played a part in setting them and this in turn will help their commitment to enhanced performance.

The objective of bringing about agreement should not blind us to the fact that it may well be necessary in the final analysis to insist on certain goals being accepted by the team member. This may be particularly necessary when performance is unsatisfactory or when in a semi-disciplinary situation. Within a good PMS, however, this should only occur on a few occasions for any manager; if it is occurring more regularly than this the manager should look at his/her own influencing skills and perhaps to the manner in which the team members are being involved in the process. Alternatively, it could be that more directive coaching methods may be required.

As a final stream of thought in respect of goal setting, managers should ensure that the goals for their team members are, where possible, fully agreed with them.

A good example of the above situation would be where a manager wished to agree a budget figure with a team member. In some organisations a budget would be 'laid on' individuals without they ever being consulted about their ability to live within such a budget while still achieving their goals. A more enlightened approach is one where the team member is consulted about the resources that are needed to meet his/her goals and where such consultation is taken into account in the setting of the final budgetary figure. If counter-arguments are developed but are not acceptable to the organisation and thus full agreement is not forthcoming then the manager's responsibility is clear; she/he must insist that the goal for that budget period remains as the criteria by which performance will be evaluated. Remember as the manager you decide whether you are communicating, consulting or negotiating and never mix the streams.

A goal setting process that absorbs the structure and qualities that we have described above will go a long way to ensuring that the organisation will derive many benefits from the process; it will also provide clear standards by which performance can be jointly evaluated by the principals involved.

It is to this review and its associated feedback processes that we now turn our attention, within Chapter 5.

Summary of Chapter 4

D E F T – Expectations of Performance

→ Clarification of Expectations is the **bedrock of a PMS**, it is the foundation on which all else is built

→ Manager and team member should maintain a **clear focus on the line of sight to the divisional/corporate goals** as the backdrop for individual/ team goal setting

→ KRAs are the **essential focus for improved performance** and success in the job role

→ Some KRAs will be **technical** whilst others will be **'soft'**

→ Goal setting within each KRA adds detail as to what is to be achieved, particularly when **insightful quantitative and qualitative measures** are included

→ From a structural viewpoint one should ensure that goals have a **beginning (Active Verb), middle (the What and the How) and an end (the Measure)**

→ Manager and team member should collaboratively develop robust goals that have **specific measures that will be motivational and allow for clarity at review stage**

→ Team members being actively involved in goal setting **increases ownership of the goal**

→ This value of joint goal setting should not deter managers from seeing that it may be necessary in some instances (hopefully a minority) to **insist on certain goals being put in place**

5

D E F T – Feedback

D – Dialogue
E – Expectations
F – Feedback
T – Timely Approach

Chapter outline
DEFT – Feedback

- → Feedback as an on-going process
- → Linking to agreed KRAs and goals
- → Preparing for the session
- → Structured format for feedback sessions
- → Tips for giving and receiving feedback
- → Exploring positive and constructive feedback
- → Commitment for follow-through

Introduction

Feedback and dialogue are essential facets of a PMS and are necessary for the leadership task of the on-going directioning of team members.

It is not really possible to give meaningful feedback without having a sound basis such as that contained within D E F T where one has identified Job Purpose, KRAs and set goals at the beginning of the review period. This earlier work becomes the foundation for interim feedback and the final feedback dialogue at the end of the review period.

Most employees welcome feedback. Indeed it is our experience that many employees are of the view that they do not get adequate feedback on their performance at work. Further evidence of this is seen in the request for satisfactory employee feedback systems, that is an oft-repeated request of employee representatives and trade unions. It is a basic fact of organisational life that most employees like to know how they are doing and how their performance is perceived and indeed noticed by their manager. This felt need within employees often provides a fertile ground for the successful introduction of a PMS.

Many managers do require some up-skilling in the process of giving both positive and negative feedback. It appears that giving honest feedback is a difficult task for many managers. Just like our earlier emphasis when talking of dialogue, this feedback process is also a joint one and some of the perceived threat within the process can be alleviated by emphasising this jointness of approach.

The principal skills involved in feedback are:

- → Reviewing performance against the goals earlier set and preparing for the Dialogue
- → Using the objective results and metrics as a touchstone but do not hesitate to refer to actual behaviours demonstrated/not demonstrated by the individual
- → Creating an environment of candor and trust, where it is accepted that no human is perfect and that we can all gain from the insights and tips that are provided for a positive purpose by others
- → Creating a collaborative dialogue, where it can be truly win/win
- → Choosing the correct amount of feedback to give. Never overload. Try and change one area at a time. It is very difficult for the performer if they are trying to change many things at once
- → Always giving feedback on specific behaviours and never referring to subjective personality issues
- → Focusing positively on real performance outcomes and on the personal development of the Reviewee
- → Listening to the performer and using the information given to decide on the leadership style that you will use in response
- → Using questioning techniques to allow the individual to cognitively explore the reasons behind success or failure

- Labelling and demonstrating how you feel about the progress of the performer
- Following-through on the conclusions of the feedback post the actual discussion.

See Panel 5.1 below for a little more detail on some these skills.

It is our experience that most managers have some or all of these competencies at their disposal but these competencies are not always used within performance management reviews. We say this because of the number of managers, team leaders and employees who tell us that the feedback processes to which they

Panel 5.1

Key Tips in giving feedback for Reviewers

- **Reviewing and Preparing:** There is no substitute for being well-prepared in advance of a performance feedback session. The foundation of the preparation is in looking back on performance (the results achieved and the behaviours demonstrated) within the review period; at this time one should have a particular focus on the goals and competencies/behaviours that were agreed at the outset. When doing this it is important to establish that one will initially ask the reviewee for their evaluation of how they have performed and plan ways in which one will get the reviewee talking as much as possible around the reasons for attainment/non-attainment; such planning will assist in making the feedback meeting one where both parties will have been fully involved.
- **Focus on Personal Development:** The performance discussion must have a component within which there is a full discussion of the personal development requirements and possibilities (competency development) for the reviewee; personal development will be treated more fully in Chapters 7 & 8. However, it is critical that the manager has a different focus of attention on development

for the top performers (A Players), good performers (B + and – Players), weak or developing performers (C Players). For example, the personal development needs of an A Player will relate to future career potential and succession planning whilst the personal development of the C Player will focus on bringing his/her performance up to an acceptable basic standard.

→ **Follow-through**: Good follow-up mechanisms are critical on those issues that have been agreed about both performance and personal development. Managers who do not deliver on promised follow-through in this regard lose the trust of their employees – and it is very difficult to regain that trust. A word of advice is to keep it simple and not try too much at once. Remember particularly that if this is a new PMS that the individual may have had several years of unstructured performance management and that trying to make up for all these deficits at once will just lead to failure. Use the pareto principle and pick the most important issues with the biggest payback and focus on these. As Jack Welch once stated to one of the authors, many companies want to have a PMS as good as GE, however, few care to understand that GE were at that time on their 17th iteration of the process.

are subjected leave much to be desired from the skill viewpoint. Therefore it is our view that not alone should managers, and their staff, focus on developing the competencies; they should also benefit from utilisation of some of the issues we raise below in respect of the structuring of the performance discussion.

It is important to develop a structural template for the manner in which one will proceed through a performance review dialogue. Such a structure would suggest that at the **beginning** one should provide a process overview for the dialogue; also one should suggest to the reviewee that towards the end of the meeting one would like their view on how you the manager are doing in providing the enabling conditions for the success of the team member's job. This latter behaviour has the benefit of the manager clearly being seen to model some open and non-defensive behaviour.

The main structural part of the review – the **middle** part - will be focused on whatever three, four or five KRAs that one wishes to focus on during the feedback session. It is critically important to emphasise the jointness of the process by inviting the reviewee to give their view of performance on some of these KRAs before the manager gives their evaluation. It is also important that the reviewer plans in advance specific ways in which she/he wishes to draw out the reviewee during the discussion; this is a particularly important aspect as failing to do this is likely to create a situation whereby the reviewer will do too much talking and the reviewee will leave without feeling quite as involved in the process as they should have been. Each area, be it positive or negative, should be explored and probed in detail. Success is seldom an accident and neither is failure. Both are caused in most cases by the behaviours used/ not used by the performer.

> Whatever the cause, it must be made clear to the individual that they own their performance and that not to perform is not an option.

If one discovers that some of the goals were not attained then one must first check to see if there were issues or events which were outside the control of the team member and which affected the non-attainment of those goals; in such instances the manager must take whatever action is necessary to remove these external impediments as soon as possible and so assure the employee.
The manager is what we call the boundary manager. He/she should be like the blocker in American Football allowing the performer to achieve the score. However, the manager has other tasks on a day-to-day basis and it is critical that the performer urgently escalates a difficulty or blockage that becomes apparent to them and does not wait until the next review and then seek an excuse that it was not his/her fault.

Of greater concern, however, are reasons for non-attainment which are within the control of the individual. In such cases the manager must explore and diagnose the possible causes of the poor performance as fully as possible and take whatever action is necessary to encourage improved performance. Such actions may involve:

→ A move to more directive coaching/mentoring

→ The provision of additional knowledge/support

- Some further training of the individual
- Direct counselling if the poor performance is continuing
- Appointment of a colleague as a buddy to assist in performance improvement

Whatever the cause, it must be made clear to the individual that they own their performance and that not to perform is not an option. It is the responsibility of the manager to be as helpful as possible to the employee in bringing about a supportive climate that will encourage the necessary changes in behaviour and performance outcomes.

Moving away from poor performance now, it should be mentioned that throughout the discussion of each of the KRAs the reviewer and reviewee should take the opportunity of focusing on future goals; these are the goals that might be required for the future review period within the existing KRAs or within new ones.
The latter part of the review discussion should draw together any personal development issues that have arisen during the earlier part of the discussion and agree actions that will be put in place in respect of such development opportunities. A common error by managers is to believe that any competency gap is best filled by training when all our experience suggests that coaching on the job is often a more suitable and effective intervention.

Before the conclusion of the dialogue the reviewer should also take the opportunity of inviting comment on how the reviewee perceives the manager in carrying out his/her coaching role for the reviewee's job. The reviewer should be at great pains to be as open as possible during such a discussion and should particularly strive to ensure that she/he maintains a non-defensive mode throughout this discussion; these should be some of the behaviours that she/he wants to see from reviewees in future discussions and it is thus important that she/he models them well themselves. Best practice in this area is that the reviewer and reviewee have a common understanding of coaching and coaching styles. This allows the reviewee to ask for the correct style of coaching to support performance issues and allows the manager to match the coaching to the performance level of the individual.

Lastly there should be an agreed summary which should include the various action points that have arisen and the required follow-up with appropriate timeframes and/or milestones. In some organisations this may also involve asking the reviewee

Panel 5.2

Key skills of feedback for Reviewees

→ **Reviewing and Preparing:**
Reviewees need to develop the skill of dispassionately examining their own performance over the review period with particular reference to the agreed goals; within this preparation they should practice the skill of reviewing: *'What went well, and why?'* and *'What could be improved, and how?'*

→ **Listening and Assertiveness:**
Reviewees need to be able to listen well in as non-defensive a mode as possible and also to be able to assert their own view of performance in a non-aggressive mode. These two skills are the basic core skills of influencing.

→ **Self-analysing:**
It is important that reviewees are capable of critical self-analysis in respect of their own performance and personal development needs. If they are so capable, they will be able to present an accurate view of themselves in a developmental context.

→ **Coaching:**
To be effectively coached the reviewee must understand the role of a coach and the styles of coaching that are appropriate to each stage of development.

to draw up a plan for how he/she will make the required changes and having this approved by the manager.

A sample template for the structuring of performance feedback is shown as Appendix II.

We now turn in Chapter 6 to the 'TIMELY APPROACH' part of our model in an effort to emphasise the importance of getting the timing right in respect of a number of aspects of a successful PMS.

Summary of Chapter 5

D E F T - Feedback

→ **On-going regular feedback** is a key requirement for a successful PMS

→ Feedback should be **firmly based on** the earlier agreed **KRAs/goals and competencies** to be demonstrated

→ **Most employees welcome feedback** on their performance, they like to know how they are doing

→ Many managers need to **improve their feedback skills**

→ It is important to develop a **climate of trust**

→ Both parties to the feedback process need to review **performance outcomes and behaviours so as to prepare well** for the feedback session

→ The **team member needs to take ownership** of the performance and personal development issues that are raised

→ Developing a **structured format for feedback sessions** – a beginning, middle and end – will greatly aid the flow of the session

→ Most feedback sessions will explore **good performance but some may need to focus on non-achievement** – in such situations possible causes need to be explored and corrective action put in place

→ The Reviewer should invite comment from the Reviewee as to the level of **support being provided through the year by the Reviewer**

→ Both parties should commit to **following-through on issues** raised during feedback sessions, thus good action-oriented notes should be made during/at the end of all feedback sessions

6

DEFT – Timely approach

D – Dialogue
E – Expectations
F – Feedback
T – Timely Approach

Chapter outline
DEF(T) – Timely Approach

- → Integrating PMS with other core organisation systems
- → Feedback should be close to the event
- → Regular reviews within PMS
- → Tips for interim and annual reviews
- → Sample timetable for phases of PMS
- → Ensuring the provision of enabling conditions for success of PMS

Introduction

The success of any PMS depends upon how well it is integrated and aligned with the other formal and informal management and HR processes in an organisation. To be effective it must become 'how we manage' rather than an 'add on' end of year process.

The true test of a good PMS is to establish your line managers response to the withdrawal of a PMS. Sadly, in many organisations the managers would be happy to be freed from the administrative chore. These are failed systems. The response in a successful PMS is 'how could we manage without this – If you take it away I will still continue the D E F T process because it is – 'how I manage'.

Various references have been made throughout earlier chapters that clearly indicate that the timeliness of feedback is very much seen as an important issue by employees.

The first alignment imperative for an organisation is to take the opportunity of integrating their PMS in a TIMELY manner with their core business cycle, such as the business planning cycle and/or the budgeting cycle. The principal advantage of this is that the PMS will be seen as well integrated in a world where often such systems are not well integrated. This also provides the vital 'line of sight' required to enable managers to lead their people by sharing context and making meaning. It will also prevent duplication of effort and will be seen by managers as an easier task.

Likewise the employees at various levels of the organisation are likely to see it as timely that the bedrock of the PMS – KRAs and goal setting – is undertaken at a time when it is synchronised with the business planning process. Thus they are likely to see that it makes sense for the goal setting process that is associated with the PMS to be implemented in a similar timeframe to such business cycles.

Various references have been made throughout earlier chapters that the timeliness of feedback is very much seen as an important issue by employees. Accordingly day-to-day operational feedback should be given as the occasion arises (close to the event) and not 'stored up' for the performance review discussion that often takes place some months later.

Even though this statement may well seem very obvious it is our experience that many managers actually do store things up for a 'rainy day', as it were. This behaviour leaves a bad taste in the mind of the reviewee who could legitimately ask why this specific feedback could not have been given at an earlier time. The de-motivating effect of such behaviour on employees

Panel 6.1

Tips for general review of performance at interim review

- Review performance achieved against goals and plans
- Explore successes and how they were achieved and learn and praise
- Explore successes and how they were achieved and learn and praise
- Explore successes and how they were achieved and learn and praise

  (The above three lines are not a typo they are a recognition that in delivering feedback most managers look to the negative much more than the positive; this can become de-motivating and reduces engagement because it lacks true balance)

- Explore performance shortfalls and how these have been created
- Review competencies demonstrated and those not demonstrated during the period
- Review effectiveness of your management and coaching of the individual during the period
- Paraphrase and agree what is the action plan moving forward for reviewer and reviewee in relation to:
  - The goals and the achievement plans
  - The competencies to be developed and the behaviours to be extinguished
  - The coaching and managerial support to be delivered
- Re-state belief in the reviewee's capability to achieve the results, to demonstrate the required competencies and highlight that this is a collaborative process

(Like all performance dialogues ensure each time that, whilst it is a collaborative process, the individual owns their own performance and the consequences for that performance.)

is incalculable and certainly can quickly bring the whole PMS process into disrepute.

There is often a lively debate about how many mini-reviews should take place during the year. It is our view that in addition to the annual performance discussion there should be formal mini-reviews on at least two or three other occasions during the year - the trend is to fit with the most common business cycle and have them quarterly. This formal mini-review need only take approximately thirty minutes but it is important to review performance in this interim way; these interim reviews also provide for checking whether or not some of the goals need to be altered in the light of emerging environmental/ organisational factors.

A further advantage of conducting such mini-reviews is that performance can be re-focused should there be a requirement so to do; thus erring performance, such as that described within Panel 6.2, can be 'nipped in the bud', as it were. On a positive level it allows for advantage to be taken of opportunities that arise as they are emerging.

As earlier stated, a key responsibility of managers is to provide the enabling conditions for success of their team members.

Mini-reviews provide opportunities for extra supports to be put in place where required at an earlier stage than at the end of the review period.

These mini-reviews can be scheduled through the year in such a manner that performance management becomes almost a continuous process, rather than a once-a-year rushed exercise. We outline in Panel 6.2 a typical best practice yearly cycle for a PMS.

Panel 6.2

Tips for review of poor performance at interim review

- → Re-focus the employee on the overall organisational goals
- → Seek employee's view of dip in performance
- → Contribute your view as to possible causes
- → Re-focus employee on original or amended goals
- → Clarify any support/ coaching that you need to provide
- → Agree further short-term review(s) of performance

Panel 6.3

A good process for a yearly cycle

Timing	Activity
October/ November	Directioning process including first two parts of D E F T – Dialogue and Expectations, whereby KRAs and goals for the forthcoming period are finalised; also discussion of personal development plan. This takes personal discipline but the reward for the organisation is that the team is ready to run onto the pitch in January. Each one knowing the game plan and their role in the game plan and how they need to change their style of play and skill level to make it happen. We have seen this approach lead to a 6% increase in efficiency in one quarter in an already top performing organisation.
March/April	Mid-year mini-review including a brief review of: → goals achieved → progress on other goals → personal development → re-directioning, if necessary? → support required?
June/July	Further mid-year mini-review including a brief review of: → goals achieved → progress on other goals → personal development → re-directioning, if necessary? → support required?
October/ November	Review of full period plus resetting of KRAs and goals for forthcoming review period.

We now move, within Chapter 7, to the issues associated with People Development.

Summary of Chapter 6

D E F T – Timely Approach

→ The success of any PMS depends upon how well it is **integrated with the other formal and informal management/HR systems** within the organisation

→ The first alignment task is to **integrate with a core business cycle**, such as the budgeting cycle

→ The PMS must become part of **'how we manage'** rather than an 'add on' end of year process

→ The **timeliness of feedback is critical** – it should be close to the event and not stored up for months on end

→ One should ideally have **two mini-reviews per year** in addition to the annual review

→ Feedback at such timely reviews should **primarily explore successes** and how they were achieved and learn and praise

→ Such timely reviews can also allow one to **'nip in the bud' any erring performance** and initiate the required re-direction in a timely manner

→ Regular reviews also allow for checking the **support that the manager is providing for performance in the team member's job**, that is the enabling conditions for successful performance by the individual/team

7

People Development Commitments

Chapter outline

People Development Commitments

→ Creating a positive climate for people growth
→ Focus on organisational needs
→ Insights on personal development within PMS
→ Alternative development opportunities within organisations
→ Integration with Organisation Training and Development plan
→ Follow-through on commitments

Introduction

On a number of occasions during the earlier chapters, and indeed in the sub-title that we have chosen for this book, we have indicated that people development is an important part of the process. Focusing on people development creates a positive climate for people growth within the PMS and in the wider organisation.

Most staff are keen to develop themselves and the PMS provides a great opportunity for discussion about an individual's personal development. A key part of successful personal development is that individuals take responsibility for their own development; they must therefore bring their development issues to the table during performance management discussions, and outside same if required. The key to this is the openness and the self awareness of the individual as well as the coaching skills of the manager.

Most personal development initiatives should be focused on organisational needs. However, one should not preclude the possibility that some personal development may be outside the current job and/or future career opportunities; therefore the discussion may look towards developing the individual in ways from which the organisation cannot have a direct immediate gain. This must always be handled very carefully as the cost of development in lost time and fees is high and an organisation in today's competitive and challenging environment must ensure that it gets the 'biggest bang for every one of its scarce training and development resources'.

In researching the effectiveness of a training and development spend in major organisations one of the authors discovered that only 20% of this spend could be clearly linked to performance enhancement. More worryingly it was also discovered that less than one in three of those who attended training and development programmes had received pre-programme briefing from their managers. This disconnect is very worrying and would not happen were there an effective PMS in place. Development is an investment but for the organisation it is a value and scarcity issue and accordingly we should only make the investment if there is a high probability of a suitable return to the organisation.

In researching the effectiveness of a training and development spend in major organisations one of the authors discovered that only 20% of this spend could be clearly linked to performance enhancement.

In a world that is now demanding performance and value, any development spend must be prioritised as follows:

- → Development required to enable the individual to complete existing role profile
- → Development to prepare individual to complete the next and more demanding role profile requirements required in the future
- → Development of A/B1 players for succession planning requirements to prepare them to be ready to progress to suit organisational needs
- → Personal development that is not connected to direct business performance or needs but will provide a more balanced and competent performance in the existing and future roles at whatever level

In order to support the development of individuals and organisational capability the PMS is uniquely placed to input to and be a two-way executive conduit for the 'Training and Development Needs Analysis' and the delivery of strategic new skill sets/ competencies to the organisation.

As part of any strategic development needs analysis it is critical that at a Strategic Human Resource Management Level the organisation identifies the new organisational skills and capabilities that are required by the organisational strategy, and which need to be deployed to deliver sustainable competitive advantage; this is usually completed at senior team level. Once these required competencies and skills are identified the reality is that these have to be learned by the relevant people with the relevant aptitudes in the specific job roles where they can make an impact. The best conduit for cascading these strategic needs is the PMS process. The Managers can then highlight the priority of these new required competencies to the key people who will be tasked with developing the new organisational capabilities. This is the strategic 'top down' value of the development aspect of the PMS process. It turns strategic capability discussions into action where real people learn and develop the skills to deliver the new capabilities.

However, the PMS is also perfectly designed to gather the 'bottom up' development needs of each individual based on their dialogue about performance, competencies and career aspirations. In essence each PMS Dialogue and Expectation Setting Meeting has the potential for producing a focussed individual learning and development plan that is integrated with strategic and operational business needs.

The development plans then need to be collated and aggregated by team/section/division and organisation so as to produce a draft organisational Training and Development plan. This then needs to be prioritised in line with budget and strategic necessities and then approved by the organisation as the Annual Training and Development Plan. This will allow the Training Department to effectively and efficiently organise the necessary multi-faceted responses and programmes.

> It is important to see personal development as far broader than the individual and/or the manager selecting a 'course' as the only significant development that individuals experience.

It is important to see personal development as far broader than the individual and/or the manager selecting a 'course' as the only significant development that individuals experience. Certainly there are many excellent development opportunities delivered through well-chosen courses; however those seeking personal development should in the first instance search for opportunities within organisations rather than outside. Development is actually 'a state of mind'.

It is about:

- → wanting to be better
- → being brave enough 'to question why'
- → exploring 'why we succeeded and why we failed'
- → asking for guidance, support and scaffolding
- → good coaching
- → being willing and wanting to change to become better at what we do and what we can do.

Managers and team members will derive significant benefit from looking for personal development opportunities for individuals in some of the ways listed in Panel 7.1 overleaf.

Competency frameworks, which we will treat in greater detail in the next chapter, are also very helpful as a language to support and guide our people development.

At the very outset of this chapter – indeed in its title – we associated the idea of commitment with personal development. We did this in an attempt to emphasise that follow-through on personal development commitments given during performance discussions (or at other times) is particularly important; we say this on the basis that employees will evaluate their manager in relation to their ability to deliver what they say they will deliver – the basis of trust building. Thus failing to deliver on such commitments has a very negative effect on the relationship between manager and team member.

Insert Panel 7.1

Development opportunities within organisations

Personal Development Opportunity	Possible Benefit
Inclusion in Project Teams, ultimately moving to leadership of same	Working with others in a focused manner; experiencing good 'project management' techniques at first hand; understanding some basic issues within change management.
Cross-functional transfers	Learning how the different roles integrate across functions and how the process flows. Gaining an understanding of the key issues that affect other units and areas.
Temporary assignments/tours of duty (This can also be outside the organisation)	Building capability to tackle more onerous projects/leadership roles. This particularly builds confidence.
Mentoring	Shares the experience of a senior executive with a new talent and provides an open space for dialogue and a sense of security for the learner.
Coaching	Develops in an agreed manner Competence, Commitment and Confidence. Enhances the role of the manager (once they are competent and committed enough to take on this role).
Executive Education	Work and learn with other executives in exploring leading edge approaches to handling contemporary issues in leadership and management.

We will now further develop the theme of people development through our treatment of Competencies within Chapter 8.

Summary of Chapter 7

People Development Commitments

→ Performance improvement can only be sustained when **people continuously stretch and grow**

→ Focusing on people development creates a **positive climate for people growth**

→ Most personal development initiatives should be **focused on organisational needs**

→ Today's world demands **performance and value**, thus any development spend must initially be prioritised towards development for **current and future organisational roles**, only then towards possible non-business development

→ The PMS should identify the **people skills required** to deliver organisational strategy and improved results

→ Opportunity should also be taken within PMS for **'bottom-up' insights** on personal development

→ Individual/team development plans should be **integrated into the organisation's Training and Development Plan**

→ Opportunity should be taken to **broaden an organisation's vision of development** so as to include activities such as **Project Work, Cross-functional Transfers, Temporary Assignments, Mentoring, Coaching, formal/ informal Executive Education and Competency Frameworks**

→ **Follow-through**, by the manager and team member, **on personal development commitments is critical**

8

Competencies: A Key Approach to People Development

Chapter outline

Competencies: A Key Approach to People Development

- → Focus on 'how' the job is to be done
- → Competency development and high performance
- → How to build Competency based approaches to People Development
- → Values for Competency Approaches
- → Coaching for Personal Development

Introduction

It seems appropriate at the outset of this chapter to give a little background prior to dealing directly with competencies. Thus we initially repeat some of the key aspects of D E F T so as to paint a context for 'bringing people on' through competencies.

Goal setting is essentially about agreeing the focus of each individual's performance. Correctly developed goals will provide 'a line of site' between an individual performer's efforts and organisational strategy. They help an individual identify clearly 'the What' of the job. 'The What' is set out in a role profile and the specific objectives to be achieved. Success or failure is measured against the achievement of objective and subjective measures. The arbitrator is the line manager.

Effective performance management exists when each individual is clear about what he/she is to achieve and how he/she is to achieve it.

It is a basic responsibility of every manager to establish the objective evidence of each individual's performance against their goals and also where judgement can only be made subjectively to make a call on the individual's achievements which cannot be so readily measured. This is not easy but it is the job of the manager. Some managers would like to simply make the measurement of every goal totally objective; however, for various reasons, most organisational performance contexts are complex and there will always be some level of subjective call that the manager must make.

However, 'the What', is only one aspect of an individual's performance; the second aspect is 'the How'. Effective performance management exists when each individual is clear about what he/she is to achieve and how he/she is to achieve it. The problem with 'the How' is that it is difficult to objectively measure (not impossible), but there are a number of core reasons why to be effective we must dissect how performance is achieved and also the behaviours that fail to produce effectiveness and efficiency in a role.

In modern professional sports environments it is the norm that plays (the How) are planned for a major game and that each player has his role and that after the game the video coach reviews with each player their individual performance in each play and identifies where the players behaviour made or broke the play. We can also see this when a professional sports coach comments in a post match environment that independent of the result he is happy or disappointed with how the team played. The 'How' is also used in professional sports psychology in focussing the players on continuing to do the right things. Players are encouraged once the game is on to ignore the score but keep doing the right things. The logic being that the scores will come.

The core reasons why we must dissect how we wish to and how we actually achieve results are that it:

→ Enables organisations to provide guidance in disseminating core values that identify what are acceptable and unacceptable behaviours in the pursuit of organisational goals. Interestingly, there are two levels to this; the first being the overarching core values/corporate culture (the super-ordinate behaviours) and secondly, the individual role behaviours. We have seen in recent corporate scandals that when 'rogue' executives fail to live to core values that the relevant firms can find themselves with serious performance issues, brand damage and lawsuits.

→ Enables managers to train, coach and develop individuals. To achieve high results we must identify the behaviours that are exhibited when performance is successful and then train, coach and develop these individuals to exhibit these success inducing behaviours and extinguish any behaviours that are dysfunctional in this context. Otherwise we are 'shooting in the dark'.

→ Enables managers who have honed their knowledge of the behaviours that are demonstrated by superior performers. This allows them to use targeted selection methods, such as competency based interviewing, to improve recruitment and succession selection. It also enables us to take a step deeper on a psychological level and identify the personality type that is most likely to demonstrate the required behaviours and accordingly be successful in the role.

We can see then that 'the How' is critical to translate corporate culture and values into guided behaviours for individuals and it is at the core of producing high performance results. As in sport we achieve high performance by doing the little things right.

Many PMSs do not fully recognise the importance of taking the opportunity of 'bringing on' the individual. However the reality is that this personal development, properly defined and integrated to the pursuit of organisational goals, is at the centre of achieving high performance at the individual, team and organisational levels.

Personal development is about developing the individual to:

1. Effectively and efficiently perform their existing role as the performance targets continually become more challenging year on year

2. Effectively and efficiently perform in the role as you expect that role to adapt in the future, for example more computerisation, legislation etc

3. Where potential has been demonstrated above to prepare them for more diverse and more complex senior positions within the organisation

4. Become generally more effective and to enable them to undertake a wide range of vocational and non-vocational activities successfully (the benefit to the organisation can be increased engagement and the more general ability of the individual to deal with more diverse job and non-job issues.

The key to unlocking 'the How' of performance is the identification of the behaviours, attitudes and skills that underpin superior performers and performance.

Competency based approaches focus on the special behaviour, attitude and skill required for superior performance in a particular role. Thus, the manager and team member will discuss and agree what are the appropriate behaviour, attitude and skill requirements in a role and strive together to improve the team member's competency in some of these areas. Discussion would be very focused on 'how' the job gets done, whereas thus far in our goals oriented focus the emphasis has been on the 'what' of the job.

The process of building competency is one of open dialogue between manager and team member. It is a positive coaching dialogue and like any sports coach the manager must know what are the behaviours, attitudes and skills that high performers exhibit and that are exhibited in high performance scenarios. It is most certainly not a process of 'ticking boxes'. Thus the manager and team member must discuss:

→ The competencies/behaviours most appropriate to the individual and their role/career

→ How the individual might enhance their own development through concentrating on the specific behaviours that will help their development in the relevant competency range

→ Discuss progress in a formal setting on the above on two/ three occasions through the year. Informally, the performer and manager will agree the coaching support required and the amount of competency reviewing required.

In order to drive home our understanding of this process let us take a sporting example. An individual soccer player and his/her coach might agree that the skill of passing might be one that the individual could improve; their discussion therefore might put together a competency range that might look something like that shown within Panel 8.1 below:

Panel 8.1

Competency Range for 'passing' the ball in Soccer

→ **Level one:**
Retention of the ball: ability to hold the ball close to one's body so that one is able to pass

→ **Level two:**
Basic passing: the skill of being able to pass the ball with right foot (being right-footed) to predetermined positions with 90% accuracy

→ **Level three:**
Basic passing: the skill of being able to pass the ball with left foot to predetermined positions with 75% accuracy

→ **Level four:**
Awareness of receivers: develop the skill of lifting one's head to survey which team member is in the best position to receive the pass and then executing the appropriate pass with 90% accuracy.

Once the coach and player have agreed a competency range along the lines within this Panel the steps along the way towards developing increased competency will be quite clear; they can focus the development of the skill successfully towards each of these levels to the point where that competency has been acquired.

Panel 8.2

Competency Range for 'Customer service'

- **Level 1**
  Aware of own personal and organisational view of the development of a quality product/service and working towards same
- **Level 2**
  Open to customers' views, when same are provided, as to how the product/service might be improved
- **Level 3**
  Proactively seeks views of customers on how best to improve the service to them in respect of existing product/services
- **Level 4**
  Proactively searches for new ways of developing newer/better products and/or services, for customers... also customer driven enhancements to existing products/services

From an organisational viewpoint competency development will usually focus on specific behaviours within some of the following four areas: job knowledge, personal effectiveness, interpersonal skills and in some cases management skills. Brief descriptions of each of these areas are presented below and outline examples of competency ranges are provided in each case.

❶ Job knowledge

Competency in the area of job knowledge puts before the job holder an increasing range of the levels of knowledge that could be acquired to better achieve results in the job. Thus the example of 'Customer Service' is shown within Panel 8.2 above.

❷ Personal effectiveness

Here we consider specific ways of increasing one's own effectiveness through skill development in particular job related areas. Such skill development is primarily achieved in job related coaching, mentoring and on-the-job assignments; formal training courses can help but the former are indispensable. An example of a competency range for increasing personal effectiveness in the area of 'time management' is shown within Panel 8.3 overleaf.

Panel 8.3

Competency Range for 'Time Management'

→ **Level 1**
Disorganised and loses opportunities due to inability to prioritise and utilise self-discipline ..... regularly back-logged.

→ **Level 2**
Inability to effectively manage interruptions (own and others) and fails to utilise more systematic approach to planning time usage.

→ **Level 3**
Well able to manage one's own time, delegates well but others still impose their priorities too regularly.

→ **Level 4**
Highly organised and capable of accommodating urgent/ important contingencies because of ability to prioritise, plan and optimise use of personal time.

Panel 8.4

Competency Range for 'Teamwork'

→ **Level 1**
Achieves personal objectives and quietly contributes to the team in small ways.

→ **Level 2**
Achieves own objectives and makes a reasonably significant contribution to team when asked for support.

→ **Level 3**
Whilst achieving own objectives searches for extra knowledge/ skill that will increase contribution to teamwork.

→ **Level 4**
Works exceedingly hard at own objectives and devising ever-improving ways to enhance own contribution to team: helps team search for collaboration within itself and outside.

❸ Inter-personal Relationships

An area of increasing importance for all employees is the enhancement of their inter-personal skills, all the more so in the light of the increasing emphasis being placed within organisations on teamwork approaches and networking. Within this category of competency development falls the identification of ever-improving ways of enhancing one's approach to inter-personal skills, as exemplified in the competency range for 'teamwork' within Panel 8.4 on the previous page.

→ Managerial Skills

As more organisations demand a greater range of managerial skills from their staff it is important for individuals within organisations to make conscious efforts to improve their managerial skills. As for each of the other categories involved there are an extensive range of skills required, only one of which is exemplified in the competency range for 'leadership style' within Panel 8.5 below.

Panel 8.5

Competency Range for 'Leadership'

→ **Level 1**
Single dimension leadership style (e.g. authoritarian) without seeing benefits of alternative approaches.

→ **Level 2**
Capable of a meaningful consultative approach on some issues, although clearly reserving all decisions to oneself.

→ **Level 3**
Focused on participative approaches, allowing for increasing involvement of team; capable of using most suitable approach for particular situations; handles group conflict competently.

→ **Level 4**
Capable of developing vision with the team, thereby enlisting them; fully committed in practice to empowering teams/team members as far as possible; takes positive steps to prevent unhealthy conflict.

Each of the above levels within each of the ranges shown can be discussed from the viewpoint of attitude, knowledge, behaviour and skill.

The above ranges are general examples. Competency ranges that are more directly related to the job and the individual's development come out of the dialogue that takes place between the manager and team member – therein lies the real benefit.

The only successful route to making these competencies personal and specific is extensive dialogue between manager and team member

All of what has been said to date has referred to competencies at the personal level. At the team/department/organisation level one can see that management teams could establish core competencies that they wish to see embodied within the local culture. Several of the above competency ranges could in fact be not alone seen at the personal level but could also be spread wider at team/department or organisation level. Thus, for example in a wider programme to establish improved communication the organisation could espouse the enhancement of the skills required for such an improvement on an organisation-wide basis. In this way then the team/department/organisation would develop a competency range and encourage individuals to move across the levels from wherever they rest at any particular time.

Competencies should not be generic. Leaving aside our earlier comments concerning team/department/organisational core competencies, an individual's competencies must be fully personalised to that individual. The only successful route to making these competencies personal and specific is extensive dialogue between manager and team member; this dialogue should centre on those behaviours that are deemed most appropriate to that person and their job/career. Such open discussion will lead to clarity about where an individual team member needs to enhance their behaviour within the competency range under discussion. **The route therefore to meaningful personalised competencies is through dialogue... and more dialogue.**

One can see from the above sample competency ranges that the differences between the competencies at one end of the range to the other are just termed 'levels'. It is important not to label same as 'poor', 'good', 'very good', 'excellent' or other labels that run the danger of categorising an individual. Develop the range with team members without such labels and encourage them to raise the level of their competency by moving across the range.

Real performance enhancement can be obtained through the personal development of individuals using the competency based approach

The establishment of a range does not imply that there are not further levels of competencies beyond what one has as the highest level at present. As an individual improves their competency and therefore moves across the competency range further discussion could actually make a new range within that competency, highlighting further ways in which that individual could develop. This is one way in which the idea of continuous learning and individual growth are bedded down within organisations.

It is important to restrict the number of competencies that individuals are focusing on at any particular time. It is our view that if one chooses about three or four one will allow for due attention to be given to those and provide the opportunity for positive re-enforcement as the individual enhances the competency.

As with all successful performance enhancement strategies it is very necessary to provide some form of coaching for the individual within a particular competency area. As the individual practices the competencies it is important that mini-reviews can take place and that further coaching be provided. Arguably this is a more important process than perhaps a training course that might temporarily add a particular behaviour/skill. Coaching on the other hand is more likely to bed down that particular behaviour/skill within the individual and the organisation.

This brief treatment of competencies should have developed an awareness of how competencies can be integrated with and enhance a goals oriented approach to a PMS. Real performance enhancement can be obtained through the personal development of individuals using the competency based approach outlined above, which we summarise on the next page.

Having completed our treatment of competencies we will now move to the difficult question of 'Linking Performance to Reward'.

Summary of Chapter 8

Competencies:
A Key Approach to People Development

→ Competency Development focuses on 'the How' – **the competencies with which one goes about carrying out one's role**

→ Focusing on 'the How' also allows organisations to **disseminate core values** and to train, coach and develop individuals/teams

→ Competency Development is at the centre of developing **high performance at the individual, team and organisational levels**

→ Competency Based Approaches focus on:
- **Attitude**
- **Knowledge**
- **Behaviour**
- **Skill**

→ **Meaningful dialogue is central** to individual development through competencies

→ Competencies can be developed in the areas of:
- **Job Knowledge**
- **Personal Effectiveness**
- **Inter Personal Skills**
- **Managerial Skills**
- **High Performance Skills**
- **Organisational Culture**
- **Technical Skills**

→ **Important values** for competency approaches:
- Competencies must be **personalised** to the current competency level of the individual/team
- Avoid the **negative effects of labelling** as much as possible
- Competency development is a **continuous process**
- Do not focus on **too many competencies** at any one time
- **Good Coaching** is required for Personal Development

→ Real **performance enhancement** and Personal Development can be obtained through competency development

9 Linking performance to rewards

Chapter 9 outline

Linking Performance to Reward

- → Linking performance and pay across an organisation
- → Complexity of pay for performance
- → Rewarding behaviours and achievement
- → Decisions on 'weighting' of reward criteria
- → Consistency and fairness of reward

Introduction

In this chapter we will describe the key issues in building an effective linkage between pay and performance.

Few organisations find it easy to develop and implement a truly effective performance reward and incentive system for anyone other than the most senior management and their sales team. This means that the majority of employees have little or no linkage between their pay and their performance.

Undoubtedly, some of this is due to mistrust of the process as paying for performance undoubtedly requires some element of subjective as well as objective decision making.

A key concept within Performance Management and Reward is that 'there is nothing as unfair as treating unequal people equally'. This concept seeks to differentiate by performance (measured by results achieved and behaviours demonstrated) and suggests that to do anything else will lead to organisational justice issues.

The greatest obstacle to this in the past has been that managers often failed to comprehend the basic principles and complexities of the process; they also found it difficult to do and thus looked for excuses not to do it.

Panel 9.1

Why pay is not linked to performance

The reason management fail to link pay to performance for many key groups is that they:

→ Do not have a clear reward strategy

→ Fail to understand the performance pay process

→ Do not have an effective performance management process in place

→ Find it difficult to measure performance for these groups

→ Lack the courage/skill or both to call individual's performance and differentiate reward. Hall, a leading Harvard Incentivisation Expert, asserts that managers who find this easy are dangerous and those who refuse to do it are not managers. He quotes Jack Welch who states that this should be hard and is hard, but it is the key role of the manager

Panel 9.2

Why Performance and Pay should be linked

- Rewarding individuals for achieving goals increases their engagement and effort in seeking to achieve these goals
- Rewarding for performance increases performance
- Differentiating reward in line with performance is fair and equitable
- Rewarding high performance behaviours increases the likelihood that these behaviours will be repeated

Practical Steps For Effectively Linking Performance and Pay

We will present 4 Steps as a means to achieving this linkage:

1. Identify the results and behaviours you are seeking to encourage.
2. Get the Performance Management process right
3. Put processes in place to ensure that managers are consistent in their decisions on performance GOALS and achievement
4. Ensure Voice, Equity and Fairness for Employees

STEP 1 – Identify the results and behaviours you are seeking to encourage.

You must know the results that your organisation sees as valuable and you must be able to prioritise those into a short priority list or scorecard at corporate level and then cascade the priority objectives list or scorecard to each Division/ Section/Team and Individual. There must be a 'line of sight' that is visible for all employees. It is the manager's job to translate and make meaning of his unit's priority objectives or scorecard and translate that into meaningful scorecards/lists to be agreed with his/her team and each individual within it. As part of this cascading we all know that all objectives even priority

Panel 9.3

Core Principles for Effective linkage of Pay & Performance

- We should reward what we value. Unfortunately a lot of firms in the words of Kerr undertake 'the Folly of Rewarding A: whilst hoping for B'
- We should reward people with what they value.
- The individual should be given an opportunity to rate their own performance
- The line manager must decide the actual performance rating
- There should be no surprise at the rating as there should have been regular performance reviews during the period
- The magnitude of the reward should be at least 20% of total salary (any less and it is difficult to motivate and differentiate)
- The decision is as objective as the goals but always involves a subjective call by the manager. Attempts to be totally objective are usually either too simplistic, too short-term or not possible.
- The reward should be as close as possible in time to the performance and the specific performance that is being rewarded must be clearly identified.

ones are not of equal importance and that the manager needs to weight them for each individual's priority list/scorecard. Once the results required are outlined there are four other important requirements that the manager must establish through answering the following four key questions:

Question 1:
To what extent do you want to link performance to incentive bonuses and/or to ongoing basic pay progression?

Some organisations use their PMS as the basis for paying variable bonuses. Others also use them to decide upon annual basic salary level increases (including pay/no-pay increments). The concept of using performance inputs for both has short term and long term advantages.

Question 2:
How much weighting will be given to individual versus team rewards?

This depends on the behaviours that are required to achieve objectives. Some organisations like to reward each individual solely based on their own objectives. This makes each individual accountable and they are incentivised to deliver their strategic contribution to the organisation; the downside of this is that it can give rise to behaviours from the employee that work against teamwork. They simply look after their own patch and do not help, and in some organisations hinder, their colleagues. If you adopt this approach and claim that you foster teamwork you are not rewarding teamwork. Some companies seek to reward the individual on a split of 25% based on team achievement and 75% based on individual contribution. This they feel is best to secure teamworking whilst also fostering individual contribution and clear accountability. There is now a trend to make this split 50:50 which really encourages the team to achieve the team objectives/scorecard whilst also rewarding the individual for their personal contribution in achieving their own goals.

Some companies seek to reward the individual on a split of 25% based on team achievement and 75% based on individual contribution.

Question 3:
How much weighting will be given to overall corporate performance?

This again depends on the behaviours you wish to foster in the organisation. Those who pay a percentage of bonus based on overall corporate performance are seeking to link the individual's performance incentive to corporate achievement; they will thus face the individual towards corporate achievement and the external market and also foster a company wide camaraderie and feeling of involvement. In such situations some percentage (often 33% and in some cases 100%) of the performance bonus will be based on corporate achievement. The downside of this approach is that those who are passengers or have not contributed or have worked against the organisation also benefit. At the other end of the continuum some performance incentives are paid only if corporate thresholds of performance are achieved; if

In making a decision on this the key question we must answer is: 'what behaviour do we wish to foster?'

these are not achieved, there is no payout. This means that an individual can achieve/earn their team and individual performance but this will not be paid unless a certain level of corporate results are achieved. The upside of this is that it clearly faces the employees to the market and external reality. The downside of this is that individuals or teams that have expended great effort and achieved the majority/all of their team and individual goals will not receive performance rewards because of what has happened in other places in the organisation or even external to the organisation. In making a decision on this the key question we must answer is: 'what behaviour do we wish to foster?'; then we must decide what is the right place on the continuum between corporate and team/individual performance pay that will incentivise the right behaviours for your organisation at this point in time.

Question 4:
How much weighting to give to results versus behaviours/ competencies demonstrated?

Our choices here lie between paying the individuals their performance incentives based on the results achieved (often seen as the most objective approach) versus the behaviours/ competencies demonstrated (often seen as subjective). However, the difficulties that can arise with just paying for results are that new/ improved competencies/processes may not be used or an individual/ team may achieve results but behave in a dysfunctional manner that damages other individuals or other teams' efforts. Likewise if the organisation is seeking to develop new sources of competitive advantage through deploying new competencies we know that if we wish to get people to focus on them we should incentivise them to use these behaviours. This again is a continuum so the choice lies with the company depending upon what it wants to achieve. Some organisations pay half of the performance incentive based on results achieved and half based on competencies demonstrated. This suggests that they equally value – What people achieve

(Pure results) and How they go about achieving it (Values behaviours demonstrated).

With increasing demands on organisations to meet ever increasing standards of ethics and compliance levels the concept of rewarding for values demonstrated as well as results is becoming more popular.

STEP 2 – Get the Performance Management Process Right

If we are to link pay to performance we must have an accepted and fair process for identifying and measuring performance and ensure that this is applied consistently across the organisation or the relevant unit of the organisation.. If you follow the steps outlined in this book, and particularly the D E F T model therein, you will have the basics for an excellent performance management system. However, when we wish to link performance to pay we must address the following or the system will damage morale or be faked:

→ We must be clear and accept that the measurement of performance is both objective and subjective. We can seldom make it totally objective and when we do there are the basic measurement difficulties of:

  a. Measuring the wrong thing
  b. Measuring what is easy to measure rather than what is important
  c. Being short term and having a tunnel vision focus which ignores the other aspects of the job
  d. Some roles are simply not easy to objectively measure because of complexity, data lag or the long term nature of the actions
  e. We must weight the reward elements

When we accept that the decision on performance achievement is both objective and subjective we can deal with the reality of linking performance to pay. If you look to the earlier chapters you will see that the performance is defined as 'The What' (the numbers and results achieved – both objective and subjective) achieved and also 'the How' – the behaviours used to achieve the results (usually subjective in nature).

STEP 3 – Put Processes in place to ensure that managers are consistent in their decisions on performance goals and achievement

This is undoubtedly one of the most difficult areas in performance management and it is critical if there is to be an acceptable and fair system of performance pay put in place. The most widely used approach to dealing with this challenge is to validate consistency through peer manager reviews and the challenging of objective setting and then a peer manager review of the performance review outcomes. Many organisations call these processes Session Cs.

It is clearly better to integrate the process if we wish to truly link performance and reward.

However, like all processes, they are only as honest as the managers that use them and they require openness and real edge/challenge. Nobody has said this was easy but it is worth doing right. Organisations often facilitate this process through use of vitality curves using an expected bell curve (normal distribution of performance across the workforce). In some organisations they force this distribution. This has the advantage of ensuring differentiation of performance but also suffers from the reality that even if one fully achieves one's own goals it is ones ranked performance versus colleagues that affects the individual reward. This is sometimes referred to as the 'rank and yank' approach. The other approach is just to use the curve as a guide and let managers argue and challenge the outcome. Again it is the dialogue that is key and managers having to make and defend their performance calls with their peers is the best way to get them to prepare for the review dialogue with their subordinates.

Step 4 – Ensure Voice, Equity and Fairness for Employees

If a performance incentive system is to be effectively introduced it must be seen as fair and just by the employees. The system must be communicated to all employees and examples of process and outcomes should be worked through with all participating employees. It is not just a management system, it is a relationship process. Once Steps 1-3 are in place their processes must be explained and an appeal process also needs to be put in place. Once the D E F T dialogue process is honest and open there will not normally be difficulties, particularly if good on-going feedback and coaching are in place.

But difficulties will arise and the employee in these cases needs to have an appeal avenue/process (this is usually to the next level manager with a special appeal mechanism to HR). It has also been established as good practice to ensure that the final scoring of the review process is not a negotiated part of the final review but rather a small and logical but critical part of the overall review and learning based on a years work. The importance of not allowing reward to take over the final review dialogue is so important that some organisations have split the reward decision communication from the performance review. It is clearly better to integrate the process if we wish to truly link performance and reward. However, we cannot allow the review meeting to be hijacked by a negotiation on performance pay. This will happen if managers are unclear about the process or are not properly trained to handle an assertive performance review meeting.

Summary of Chapter 9

Linking Performance to Reward

- → Few organisations find it easy to **successfully link performance and pay** across the organisation
- → Managers have found it **difficult to grasp the complexities** of pay for performance and have thus often looked for excuses not to do it
- → Get the PMS working well **prior to linking it to pay**
- → Rewarding individuals/teams for achieving their goals increases their **engagement and effort**
- → Rewarding high performance behaviours increases the likelihood that **such behaviours will be repeated**
- → The magnitude of the reward should be at least **20% of total salary**
- → Clarify your thoughts on the **weighting** to be given to individual, team and corporate achievements and also the weighting to be given to competencies demonstrated
- → Put processes in place to ensure **consistency of the management of performance and pay**
- → Ensure **Voice, Equity and Fairness** for Employees
- → **Managers get the behaviours that they reward**

10

Critical success factors for D E F T

Chapter outline
Critical Success Factors

→ Role of top management
→ Line of sight to Organisation goals
→ Integration of PMS with Organisation systems
→ Participative dialogue
→ Quality Feedback skills
→ Best practice coaching and training
→ Consistency of application
→ Regular recognition of good performance
→ Personal development
→ Managers 'make the call'
→ Excellent follow-through mechanisms

Introduction

Having looked in detail at the various elements within a goals oriented and people development PMS it is necessary to dwell for a moment on the following essential commitments and behaviours that are vital if full organisational benefit is to be derived from such a system.

1 Role of Top Management

Full commitment from the top management team is a pre-requisite for success. This is not to be any form of lip service but a full-blown commitment to the objectives and all of the implementation stages of the system. **The Chief Executive and his/her senior staff need to be, and be seen to be, the designers and drivers of the system.** Thus, it should not be a Human Resource Department driven system; it must be owned by line management and driven by them at the most senior level. **Commitment is demonstrated through a set of behaviours that are clearly seen to be totally supportive of PMS as a line management system.**

The senior management team demonstrate this commitment particularly through:

- **Modelling best practice performance management behaviours themselves** in the manner in which they use the PMS and thus spread these best practice behaviours across the organisation
- Taking most seriously the task of **providing the enabling conditions for the success of the system** and for the success of the jobs of individuals and teams within the organisation

A further important role for senior management is that of ensuring that each succeeding layer of the organisation monitors the achievement of the next layer with specific reference to how they are carrying out their role within the system. This is best achieved by actually making the proper operation of the system a Key Result Area for each manager; thus they will be evaluated in a detailed manner on their efforts to operate the system when taking part in their own performance dialogue. Therefore, if any individual manager is not operating the PMS in the required manner this will be picked up quickly and corrective action can be taken.

2 'Line of Sight' to Organisation Goals

If the PMS is to contribute to organisation effectiveness then a clear 'line of sight' must be maintained to the strategic direction and goals; failure to maintain this will leave the PMS operating in a vacuum.

This 'line of sight' connection to the organisational focus provides the context and backdrop for the setting of tightly measured individual and team KRAs and goals, which are the foundation of the PMS.

The Joint agreement of these KRAs and Goals, which we have earlier stressed, will greatly aid individual/team ownership and provide a motivational platform for future performance; management must work hard at attaining this jointness of agreement in the vast majority of situations.

❸ Integration

The success of a PMS is greatly enhanced if the operation of the system is **timed to integrate with other systems within the organisation,** such as for example linking the KRA and goal setting process to the planning and budgetary cycles.

The process of PMS should also be integrated in the management style of the organisation, whereby **it should become more the 'way we manage around here' rather than an add-on process.**

❹ Participative Dialogue and Team Member Participation

Designers of PMS should focus the attention of all participants on the importance of open and trusting dialogue rather than the usual emphasis on forms, which are only a means of focus and recording. Too often, however, they become the focus of the process and in fact can then get in the way of satisfactory performance review.

Best practice dialogue skills require that all parties come to the dialogue in as non-defensive a mode as possible.

Many earlier Appraisal or Evaluation systems were such that the manager often carried out the evaluation of the employee without the employee knowing what were the criteria for evaluation and without he/she playing any part in the evaluation process. The results of such evaluations were most often not even discussed with the employee in question. Such systems are usually described as 'closed' systems; they do not work effectively.

An essential feature of effective systems is that they be 'open' systems whereby there is a very high level of team member involvement at all stages of the process. Thus all employees included within a goals oriented system should be involved in the process of setting the goals for their own future performance, the review of that performance and the performance dialogue that would ensue with their manager.

Having an open PMS removes one of the criticisms of older

methods of 'appraisal' whereby staff asserted that the process was a secret one in which they had no involvement. The fact that they now have involvement helps them to become committed to the total process and in particular to the goals that are mutually agreed.

Finally, a high level of team member involvement increases the likelihood of reaping the benefit of improved communication between the manager and team member to which we referred earlier.

❺ Quality Feedback Skills

Most employees welcome feedback on their performance and this **feedback should be firmly based on the earlier agreed KRAs and goals and additionally on those aspects of Personal Development that are for review.**

The aim of the Feedback is a joint open collaborative process focused on performance improvement. This aim is best achieved by maintaining an emphasis on individual/team and organisational learning. Learning to learn is at the core of the high performance organisation.

❻ Best Practice Coaching and Training

We have earlier stressed the need for managers to build on the above-mentioned Feedback process and to develop across the organisation excellent coaching skills; **such coaching skills will allow them to bring the best out of employees. The development of positive coaching skills is a key enabling condition for the success of a PMS.**

In addition to coaching, one of the critical aspects of the PMS that is quite often either totally omitted or only given scant attention is the question of training for those who are going to be involved in the system.

This training needs to be on two levels. The first is one of understanding the various elements within the system and this can be readily put across in a knowledge based meeting or other intervention. The second, however, goes beyond the level of understanding as it attempts to develop within individuals the skills that are required to successfully operate the system.

The principal skills that are required for a goals oriented/people development system are:

a Identifying Key Result Areas

b Goal Setting

c Coaching and counselling skills for Performance Discussions

Many effective short training courses are available that will substantially improve the skills of managers in these areas; however it is our belief that these skills are best bedded into an organisation by having the skills input as part of normal weekly, monthly management meeting. Having skill sessions within such meetings will re-inforce the value that skills development is a key essential part of the job and will also have the decided benefit that the team, whilst being trained together, are achieving consistency in respect of the optimal implementation of the system.

It is vitally necessary for an organisation to realise that it must invest in skill development when introducing a PMS. When such skill development takes place managers and staff are better equipped for the demands of a PMS and thus they can be more certain of attaining their objectives out of the system.

7 Consistency of Application

One of the recurring problems that bedevils PMSs is different standards of application across the organisation. Different managers apply the system in a manner whereby employees are able to see inconsistencies.

This consistency of approach is most particularly required in ensuring that:

→ All departments and managers buy into the values of the PMS and consequently ensure that they themselves and their team members take it seriously.

→ The measures put in place are both stretching and of similar degrees of difficulty of attainment across the organisation

→ At the review stage similar performance yardsticks are being applied across different groupings of employees

→ The outcomes of the PMS should be consistent with the outcomes of other processes such as the Reward System, particularly in the situation where there may not be a definite linking of PMS with the Reward

It is, therefore, necessary that an organisation's senior team keeps a very active eye on the subsequent levels

of management so as to monitor their consistency in the application of the system. Even though at times this 'auditing' function is troublesome, it is in the long run beneficial for the organisation as the system will be a fairer one and will be seen to be so.

❽ Regular recognition of Good Performance

Successful managers are fully aware of the motivational benefits of recognition for staff when a job is well done. This reference is not to money. It is to the many alternative ways that a manager can encourage employees by clearly demonstrating pleasure with good job performance; this can be done in small ways such as:

→ **Acknowledging that the job was well done by word and gesture, all the better if in public**

→ **Seeking ways to give additional responsibility**

→ **Building on earlier successes to demonstrate progress and instil confidence**

→ **Writing a short note/email of thanks and encouragement.**

Managers who make behaviours like these a part of their normal management style are aware that such behaviours are a far more powerful motivator than money itself – rewarding individuals for achievement increases engagement and effectiveness.

❾ Personal Development

Personal Development must primarily be focused on organisational needs – current roles and potential future roles. Personal Development should also be linked to future skill needs that emerge from the organisational strategy.

Personal learning opportunities are many and varied and organisations should not just focus on Training as being the only or best option; perhaps better development can derive from Project Work, Cross-functional Teams, Mentoring, Coaching and Executive Education, among other methods.

❿ Managers 'make the call'

Whilst we strive to be as objective as possible, there is always a subjective aspect in reviewing the performance of another person. It is the role of the manager to make this 'call'. It is not easy, but it is management! No manager can avoid this reality without letting down the organisation and his/her people.

11 Excellent Follow-through mechanisms

It is vital that organisations impress upon all who are involved in PMS, particularly managers, that it critically important to have good follow-up to ensure that the good planning and execution that goes into the system can be followed up at the appropriate time.

This is particularly important in respect of commitments given by managers in the areas of support that is required of the team member and also in respect of building on commitments given during Personal Development discussions.

Failure to follow-through leaves a sour taste with the employee and damages the level of trust that should exist between manager and team member.

Organisations that wish to take PMS seriously must take account of the above critical success factors if they want to attain both the objectives of the system and the benefits that can be derived from its successful implementation and operation.

Conclusion

Finally, organisations intent on achieving success need to create a culture that will value achievement. The **D E F T** model of Performance Management that we have described in this book facilitates the creation and maintenance of such a culture. It does so by bringing about a performance focus that is results oriented. Employees will see the effects of focusing on key aspects of their jobs and benefit from the regular feedback and positive coaching process involved in this system. The organisation will see enhanced performance from individuals as they become accustomed to the process. All of this helps to build the required performance and achievement culture.

Help your organisation achieve these benefits by encouraging your management team to take Performance Management seriously.

Now... start with yourself and your team... good luck!

Summary of Chapter 10

Critical Success Factors

1. Firm 'behavioural' commitment from top management
2. Maintain 'Line of Sight' to Organisation Goals
3. Integration of PMS with other organisational systems
4. Dialogue and high level of team member participation
5. Quality Feedback Processes
6. Best Practice Coaching and Training
7. Consistency of Application
8. Regular Recognition of good performance
9. Personal Development
10. Managers 'make the call'
11. Excellent Follow-through mechanisms

Working hard to do all these things well will greatly facilitate the development of a performance management culture throughout the organisation.

Appendices

A

Appendix I

Template of Simple Performance Management 'Form'		
Key Result Area	GOALS Active verb... 'What' is to be achieved and the 'How'... Measure	Progress Through the Year

Appendix I

Developmental Focus on Competencies/Skills (Develop a stepped developmental range for two competencies/skills related to current/future job)		
Agreed Developmental/Training Needs (Identify some development opportunities for current job and/or future career)		
Additional Comments		
Signature:	Signature:	Date:

Appendix II

Sample Template for the Structure of Performance Discussions

Beginning

- → Set a warm tone and a climate of helpfulness and positive coaching
- → Provide an overview of the structure of the session
- → Indicate that at the end you would like some feedback on how well you are providing the support that the team member requires

Middle

- → The main portion of the session will be given over to a discussion of the earlier agreed KRAs/Goals with clear 'line of sight' to organisational goals
- → Attention must also be given to how the team member has been achieving these KRAs/Goals – the behaviours demonstrated to others and the contribution to teamwork
- → Positive behaviours and achievements must be praised
- → Personal Development and Competency Development should be discussed in the context of current needs and the on-going strategic needs of the organisation

End

- → Re-cap in a positive coaching manner on the main outcomes of the session
- → Invite now a discussion of your own delivery of the required support to the team member
- → Warmly thank the team member for their performance during the review period

Notes

Notes